Mulroney & Others

Books by Baron Wormser

Mulroney & Others

POEMS

Baron Wormser

Sarabande  Books

LOUISVILLE, KENTUCKY

Managing Editor
Sarabande Books, Inc.
2234 Dundee Road, Suite 200
Louisville, KY 40205

LIBRARY OF CONGRESS CATALOGING-IN-PUBLICATION DATA

Wormser, Baron.
    Mulroney & others : poems / by Baron Wormser.
        p.   cm.
    ISBN 1-889330-38-8 (cloth : alk. paper). — ISBN 1-889330-39-6
(pbk. : alk. paper)
    I. Title.   II. Title: Mulroney and others.
PS3573.O693M84   2000
811'.54—dc21   99-23169
                                                                            CIP

Cover Art: *The Congregation* by Mario M. Muller. Courtesy Elizabeth Dee
Gallery, New York, NY.

Cover and text design by Charles Casey Martin.

Manufactured in the United States of America.
This book is printed on acid-free paper.

Sarabande Books is a nonprofit literary organization.

for Arthur Chesley

Acknowledgments

I wish to thank the John Simon Guggenheim Memorial Foundation for the fellowship that helped me to complete this book.

Grateful acknowledgment is made to the editors of the following publications, in which these poems first appeared, sometimes in different versions:

American Letters and Commentary: "Zbigniew Herbert's Mr. Cogito Meets Emily Dickinson: A Literary Romance"

Artful Dodge: "Fatality"

DoubleTake: "Route One-Thirty"

5 AM: "Meditating (New England, 1892)," "Bobbin' "

Hubbub: "O Mother Europe (1931)"

The Kenyon Review: "The Great Depression," "Imagining Napalm: Harvard Square Summer (1967)"

Limestone: "Acting Out"

Maine Times: "January," "In the Grocery," "The Haircut," "Schoolhouse Blues"

The Manhattan Review: "For the Yiddish Poets," "MIA—Missing in America," "In the Country of the Pointed Firs (1972)," "Portrait of the Artist"

The Massachusetts Review: "Goethe in Kentucky (1932)," "Melancholy Baby"

Michigan Quarterly Review: "For Jane Kenyon," "Spirits of the Mall"

The New Republic: "A Roman"

Notre Dame Review: "Bernard Baruch"

River City: "Immolation (1964)," "Draft Morning (1969)"

Solo: "Poem for My Son"

Synaesthetic: "Furniture"

Tar River Poetry: "Mulroney"

Tennessee Quarterly: "Kid"

Table of Contents

Mulroney & Others

Mulroney

Where the hell do these people come from?
Mulroney asked me.
We were crumpling up a Sunday *New York Times*
That had found its way into the pile of papers
We used as packing filler for glass jars of honey.
We were wadding up the wedding notices—
Young lawyers in love with account executives.
Their fathers were surgeons and vice-presidents;
Their mothers were psychologists and counselors.

We were working as prep cooks at a ski resort
And packing boxes at a place down in the valley
To make a couple extra bucks.
Mulroney didn't know anything except
Eat, fuck, sleep, ski. A regular physical guy,
He barely knew what Vietnam was
And it was 1975.
He could have lived any time, any place,
And for all ostensible purposes he was.
He'd wake up in the morning in the cabin
We shared and it was cold and he'd curse
And try to coax whatever woman he was sleeping
With to start the fire in the woodstove.
I could hear him cooing in his gravelly
Flattened brogue of a voice.
A few mornings the woman would get up, most
Mornings not. Defeats and victories and
Sunlight licking the frosted windows
And Mulroney full of the dumb sap of time
And scratching his balls.

Where the hell do these people come from?
He asked me.
Mulroney, you dim honky ass, I said.
They are groomed to run the show
And he looked down at the crumpled vivacity
Of the young brides in newsprint
And he broke into an almost lovely smile
And he said in a voice that could have
Passed for thoughtful, How sad.

2

The Tape

Around eleven-thirty Al's fallen asleep
And you zap the TV with the remote
Because late night has never been your thing,
Those smiles like new clothes,
Those voices like prom kings and queens
As if every night were the big date.
You have to wonder about people
So eager to talk about themselves.
Probably nothing much has happened to them,
They were too busy smiling.

You put on the videotape of Claudia
Cooking in her eighth grade Home Ec class,
And she's wearing a blue corduroy jumper
That could have been hemmed better,
And she's got on those dingy braces that
Doc Eastley claimed would do the trick
But it doesn't matter much what Doc thought
Because Claudia was in that car that
Sheila Hersheimer who was all of sixteen
Was driving that strayed across the center
Line (as they said in the newspaper) into
The path of a one-ton Chevrolet truck.

What the hell do you do this for?
Aren't your nights harrowed enough already?
Aren't your eyes sick with seeing
The same thing over and over?
Isn't your soul so dismal that getting up
In the morning is more like a dream than a life?
Of course you know the answer—
She's alive on that tape and that's what

You want to feel, her being alive.
It's not complicated and it's not as wrong-
Headed as the therapist says it is
Because you know she's dead and you can
Feel her spirit leaving yours little by little
Each day, a real slow seepage,
Like summer turning into autumn.
The tape seems to stop that,
The tape is a slap in your stupid face.

Al's snoring. His sinuses
Are getting worse. Probably you should move south.

You stop the tape, stare at the blue screen
For a while, hear your own strangely rapid breathing.
We're born ignorant and we build on that,
You think. The tape will break one of these days.
God will fall from the sky one of these days,
Yet some part of you is happy—
As if you had just met someone you hadn't seen
In a long time and had found some true feeling
That had been lost. Some part of you is happy to feel
The tingle of a child's life.

You turn on the TV and some guy
With every hair neatly in place, as if it were
A dried grass arrangement, is telling a story
About an ex-wife. Or maybe it's an ex-life.
You used to be a believer too in your way.
And when you close your eyes you see a girl
Holding up a wooden spoon and twirling it
Like a baton.

4

Zbigniew Herbert's Mr. Cogito Meets Emily Dickinson: A Literary Romance

The minuet of extroversion is not exquisite.
Although Mr. Cogito has taken lessons from
A dancing master prosperous enough to maintain
A studio in a respectable neighborhood,
He distrusts the patterned movements of balls.
Formal pleasure is not genuine pleasure, he feels.
Meanwhile, the vagaries of the gentry are encyclopedic.
The pursuit of delight is an ordeal.
Mr. Cogito's shoes pinch.

He prefers to dance with a ghost.
She is curiously halting, angular,
Her witticisms have a distinctly metaphysical cast.
Her tokens of favor include a clump
Of cat hair, an itchy mitten, a murmur,
Her smile is beautifully homely.

Mr. Cogito is the object of derision and compassion.
A countess invites him to lunch.
Her gloved hands inveigle his.
A large landowner with a hirsute voice invites
    him to shoot grouse.

Mr. Cogito hears the rustle of fearless skirts
A moth in winter
A candle breathing.

He begins to write verses on scraps of paper
Broken epigrams
Spendthrift metaphors.

He refuses the last dance
As a young woman whirls through the mazurka
With a gallant young captain.

Mr. Cogito stares out a window
Into the night.
Soon he will be home in his
Little room, a book in his hands,
Pursuing heaven and earth.

Goethe in Kentucky (1932)

Imagine (my mother said) two German Jews
Plunked down in Kentucky in the 1930s:
Mules and Model T's and consonants
Like banjo twangs and that brown tobacco
Dribble that was so intensely disgusting.

Imagine Herman and Clara and their two suitcases:
No silver candlesticks to celebrate Shabbos,
No leatherbound books, no Goethe
That all-purpose sage-artist who equably
Plumbed the demonic channels of human casuistry
Yet sang like a cheerful Greek bird,
Who loved Italy and his bit of Germany.

Imagine Goethe in Kentucky and you can see
Some of what it must have been like for
Herman and Clara, how they looked around
Timidly and boldly, knowingly and unknowingly,
Since this was the same earth and same people
But transposed into another key.

Imagine them learning to go about
Their American business beneath
A soft spring sky lacy with little clouds
And a sky dark as a hellfire preacher's Bible
And a sky blank with the torpor of summer.

Imagine them sitting at a kitchen table and puzzling out
The racial laws that applied to Negroes but in various ways,
As the infamous Christ-killers, also applied to them.
Imagine the dance of deference and hate, the faces
Opaque as window shades, the shades of meaning

Barbing the simplest words, the baffling Mandarin
Etiquettes, and the occasional howl of petty or
Major violence that bayed for a day or two before
Sinking like a dream into the sun of morning.

Imagine Goethe there at some crossroads in Kentucky
Looking at a tree or a church or a car
And shaking his beautiful radiant head that loved
This world so deeply and him being thankful for his life
In this land that was so large it could swallow like
A scrap of toast the rankest, most festering insanity.

Junior High

My buddy Jimmy Pappas sat over by
The windows where he claimed the glare
Blinded Mrs. Dagmar who would forget
That Jimmy was in the room. "The Twilight
Zone," Jimmy called it. The sun only worked
That way for around a half-hour but
It was better than nothing and allowed
Jimmy to read Plutarch and *Mad* magazine
In relative peace. The Romans were experts
At political mayhem. We were Boy Scouts compared
To the Romans. It depressed me that the Romans
Had one up on us, as if the human spark
Were wearing down. "Perfection is like
Paradise, it doesn't exist," Jimmy said.
What a sententious little fuck he was.
Marcy Goldfarb's breasts straining
Against her peach-colored jersey seemed
Perfect enough to me but I kept that topic
To myself since I had glasses and braces,
Was overweight, and would never get to
First base with her. I sat at my gouged out
Wooden desk—"Dagmar eats it," "J.W. loves
B.T."—and compiled enemy lists like
A little Richard Nixon though unlike Dick what
Enticed me was mercy not revenge.
In my mind some kid would plead about how
He didn't mean to torment me on the playground
Or Marcy would be glad to go out
With me or Mrs. Dagmar would
Give me extra credit for making witty asides
Behind her back and I'd say, "It's okay.
Just go on being who you are. You don't

Have to be good." Jimmy told me I was
Nuts and that I talked to myself
Under my breath like some old guy sitting
On a bench with a pint in a paper bag.
"Time buries all things," Jimmy opined.
Mrs. Dagmar droned, Marcy yawned
And stuck her chest out, I pardoned
Yet another worthless, eager slime.

(for David Keller)

Niagara

After it was over—"it" being
Nine married years of mingled yet resonant feelings—
He found himself revisiting places
They'd been—not for the sentimentality or
The narcotic of habit but to feel
The consolations of durable reality, to grasp
However clumsily that, yes, they had eaten at
The Hawaiian Garden in the small shopping center
Beside the elementary school and had sat
At that table near a fountain that burbled
Politely if not musically or that they had stood
In the lobby of a cavernous movie theater and
Made conversation about work or fixing
Up the living room or whether to buy popcorn or not.

Was there anything glibber than time?
It was like the bottle redemption center
Where you counted empties. You came up
With a number but what you were counting had
Nothing left in them. They had gone into you and become
Part of you but that organic wisdom was little help to one who
Yearned for some handhold on a Niagara of impudent moments.

"I am but I was. . . ." He pondered that construction
As he strolled the pebbly path in back of the condo.
No wonder (he thought) that people love money so much.
He felt he understood what a miser was—
A hoarder of stunted feelings.

He looked at photographs—those coins of instants
Spilling from wallets and purses and testifying to

The throb of solidity. Though no one was watching,
He surreptitiously put them away.

                                      One night he found
Himself in the local library and was surprised—it wasn't
A place they'd gone to. He sat for the better part of an hour
At a computer screen and looked at headlines that weren't
That old—ten years—but already seemed quaint with
The incapacity and indifference of age.

                                          There is nothing:
He could feel the void within him like a spoon
In his mouth or a chill on his flesh, not a scary feeling
More like a terrifying calm, the serenity of a blank screen.
He rose cautiously, afraid that he or the machine
Or the library might break beneath the zero weight.
He walked home slowly, lost in no thoughts.
Nine years . . . and he could touch the loss within the relief.

Briefly

To stand and drop
Or toss or let fall any little available
   object
Into water.

To throw slush into an April stream
And gape at that soft second when semblance
   dissolves
Or spit into a puddle
Or skip a pebble on a pond
Or let a stone plummet
Or allow a bit of fluff to drift in the wind
   and
Eventually, out of the eye's reach but not the mind's,
   kiss the river below
Or scuff a bit of bark or moss or duff
   into
The thin ditch beside the road
Is to be seized by the plight of vertiginous
   wonder.

The hand that lets go
Seems godlike
          and the pang of that moment
When some minute presence
              is borne away for good
Is dizzying
As the dry beech leaf rides
           and bobs and darts
Or the snow turns gray
         in the water and is gone
And the awful assumption of death

And the illusion of anything
                    being fixed in time
Are tangible
          and briefly imaginable.

In the Country of the Pointed Firs (1972)

"The process of falling in love at first sight
Is as final as it is swift in such a case,
But the growth of true friendship may be
A lifelong affair," or so the last century said as
I sat reading in the chill, dour parlor
Of a New England farmhouse in the first
Year of my youthful marriage.
                              Above my head
My wife lay on our bed reading her novel.
We cooked, made love at random hours,
And read feverishly through that stern winter.
We looked out the mullioned windows for what
Seemed like hours as if hoping for a sign
From a time of year distinguished by weeks
Of nagging flurries.
                      We quivered like squirrels
And read as if to take our temperatures, as if
To proclaim a second- or third-hand sanity since
Our own was suspect. "This will last," we proclaimed
To one another as we made soufflés for six and
Sat down at our little table set for two.
Wan, plaster walls and plain, pine floors—the quiet
Weight of other lives assailed us. Had they
Been happy in love? Had they on another
Frozen, February day dared to ask
For something more than salt or sugar?

Snow ticked at the panes, we read on,
Enthralled by other worlds, hoping our own
Would neither combust nor pall.

Schoolhouse Blues

It'd rain and the Knowles twins
Wouldn't show up. Their mother'd
Write a note that it'd rained that day—
As if they were sugar cubes.
I could understand it though,
Their hearing the drumming on the roof
And not wanting to go through
The dailiness under those
Imperfect circumstances, preferring
To stay in their beds, eat a late
Breakfast, watch TV, enjoy the warm
Nothingness of a day at home.

As their teacher I was sick
With caring, sick with attentiveness,
Sick with the graded gist of every
Fraction and word and beleaguered look.
My skin seemed to be hardening
Into armor. I had no thoughts
Beyond the next morning's lesson.
Who wanted my solicitude and
Who wanted the mumbo jumbo
Of apportioned knowledge? Weren't
The hours ruly enough already? It
Rained; the Knowles twins stayed home.
They'd never graduate. *Do we have*
To do this? Every day it rained.

In the Grocery

It's been around ten years since I'd seen
Tammy LaChapelle but I knew it was she
Standing in front of the dry cereals, not that
She was anyone special as a student—
"Special" means "special" which means one
Or two a year—but she read the books I told
Her to read and she wrote the papers.
She liked the Emily Dickinson poems we do
Every year but high school becomes history fast
And when I look in her face it's plain
That it hasn't been an easy decade:
There's a hardness in her eyes and around her lips
As if you couldn't buy a deep smile from her
And I know that story too well—when she
Was eighteen her boyfriend was twenty-five and she
Was riding around in a man's truck and she was balling
A man—not some schoolboy—every night that
She could sneak out of her house and she was a woman—
Adored, irresistible, and available.

That must have gone to hell the way it usually does—
Him getting edgy and her getting bored and there'd be
Another and another but she's always on her own, she's
Always alone even when a guy's right inside her
And she doesn't know what's going on because it's her
Raw body that turns them on like lights
And somehow she's more than that body.

It's not that I'm shrewd, it's that I've known
Twenty Tammies. I want to say that sex is a gauntlet
More than a blessing and I notice the little girl
Behind Tammy, blond and wary, as Tammy says,

17

"Hi, Mr. Wormser." We stand there flat-footed for a few
Moments as we trade harmless inquiries and
There's a pride in her voice that says it's her life
No matter what and she's not apologizing to anyone.

We both turn to the boxes of flakes and oats
And we both look hard at them so as not to look
At each other and there are tigers and elves
And smiling children on the box fronts and we each
Pick up a box deftly and carefully as if we were big
And we were making a grown-up choice.

After Midnight

The year the Goodwins gave their only New Year's Eve party
Town wisdom had it that Frank was about to start
His own firm and that Louise had taken a lover.

They stood in the doorway of their stenciled colonial hall
And greeted each guest warmly: Frank, hale yet shrewd,
Louise in a little black dress they used to call "slinky."

Two white-brick fireplaces flamed authentically
As the partygoers dismissed another parcel of time.
The chaste walls grew loud with sanguine chatter.

After midnight, they swapped small confidences:
The men about their prospects and companies,
The women about children and married uncertainties.

The fire collapsed to a flicker of embers.
Cups and words lingered on people's lips
Like long-pondered memories.

No one winced or paced or feared that such murmurs
Were culpable. Why would they? The cruelty of art,
The clarity that skewers the ready complaisance

Of consciousness had no place on that cold night
In that dreamy, wainscoted den. The promise of another
Chance was, for a few hours, childishly enticing.

Across the room Frank and Louise exchanged
Emboldened winks as if they were actors or friends.

Imagining Napalm: Harvard Square Summer (1967)

Neither the sky nor the succulent earth
But the sticky sizzle of asphalt,
Honking fumes,
The ratcheting clack of redoubtable trolleys,
Empty wine jugs set on walls, car roofs, and statues of
Puritan divines, the vast declarative sea of ambling youths.

Revolution was inspired frustration
Or the playacting of fashion.
Ardor, a bare yet grandiloquent stage.

The harridan Irish landlady
Her right eye buried by a stroke
Screamed through the locked door,
"Who's in there with you? Your whore?"

The workers appeared each morning in their
    awkward uniforms
To stand behind counters and manage machines.
When handed a leaflet, a Negro woman
Smiled at it and said sweetly,
"Honey, you don't know shit."

A professor with lacquered gray hair
Admitted on one, fresh, after-the-rain morning
That she loved Immanuel Kant.
Someone belched pacifically as she
    smiled at herself,
Serene in her dutiful clarity.

Imagining napalm while lacing up
One's sneakers, removing a Band-Aid,
Noticing sparrows revel in the litter-strewn hedges,
Waiting in line to see a foreign movie.
Imagining napalm—the jelly burn, the reek ...

Staying in bed all morning, reading Marcuse and
Mainlining the radio's guitar-chanting glory.

"In the West, what we call karma,
You call history," a tall man
With a kind, thin face preached
To a gallery of proto-mystic explorers.

Standing in the warm breath of the summer night
And staring at the dark, filthy river.
Thinking about the other side of the world,
Some guy suddenly screaming and falling.

Imagining napalm and arguing long-distance
On the phone about the war and obliviously
Licking the sweet, intricate moment of an ice cream cone.

Angel of Death

Angel of Death pays us an impromptu visit.
That's what we call him,
He's a mycologist.

We start talking about how light
    death is,
Light as a pepper flake,
    a plum blossom petal,
    a cat hair,
    a cell.

We shake our heads in disbelief
That the beautiful, animate, babbling body
Becomes a rotting stone.
We know that everyone has been shaking
Their heads forever this way but still we do it too.

We're getting older and we're not as keen
About distractions as we once were.
We want to see clearly as long as we're here.

Angel of Death is tall and gawky
But when he strides through the woods
He's lovely as he stoops down and brushes
Away some duff and plucks a mushroom.

Light as a syllable,
    a sigh before falling asleep,
    a bubble,
    a spore.

The Haircut

Dwayne Richardson'd been growing
This Beatle hairdo that looked pretty
Dorky on him because his hair wasn't lank
And fine but more like a wavy wire brush.
One day grew into another until the principal
Invited Dwayne in for a chat (as he liked to put it)
And said he was going to suspend Dwayne if
Dwayne didn't get rid of that silly long hair.
It was an issue of honor and Dwayne said, "No, sir,"
In a voice of deferential defiance.

During his week off, Dwayne hiked down to the recruiter's
Office in Portland and joined the Army.
He was in 'Nam in what seemed like no time
And no one thought much about him and then he was dead.
It was sketchy as to how it happened but he wasn't coming
Back alive and the principal said on the loudspeaker
One day that we'd lost a hero. By that time
The Beatles were starting to get pretty weird as
Were a lot of other people and later Dwayne's sister
Patty said that another grunt in the platoon told her how he
And Dwayne used to smoke a bone some nights for their nerves
And talk about high school and music.

The first thing the Army had done was cut his hair.
"Irony is the oxygen of modern times," Mr. Hamilton,
The smartest of the four history teachers, used to say.
Maybe Dwayne didn't have him or if he did he was looking
Out the window at the sunshine when the teacher said it
Or he was humming "A Hard Day's Night" in his head or
He heard it quite distinctly and wrote it down in his notes
And paused and thought.

23

Bernard Baruch

When I was a boy, people were always talking about
　　Bernard Baruch the Wall

Street wizard who unofficially advised presidents,
　　made a fortune for himself and sat

On a park bench from whence he tossed his wisdom
　　upon the queasy tides of human events.

He was always in the newspapers
　　where his considered yet snappy quotes

About how to give everyone a share
　　in the pie called "America" made

First-rate, things-are-looking-up copy
　　and he was always being photographed

On that park bench, an urbane yet somehow bucolic
　　philosopher who was securely rich

And hence credible because a poor man couldn't
　　have known much—if he did he would

Have been a rich man. When the wizard died
　　there were various encomia,

Though not from my Uncle Sidney who, though he'd never
　　met the gentleman, pronounced Mr.

Baruch a self-important windbag whose notion
　　of civic virtue had more to do

With preserving the prerogatives of finance capitalism
   than altruism.
                     Sidney was an intelligent

But embittered schoolteacher who wanted to become
   a trial lawyer but owing to

The circumstances of the Great Depression
   found himself spending his

Life appraising tenth graders' inchoate essays about
   Machiavelli and Pericles.

When Sidney died there were no telegrams from
   politicians, corporate titans,

Or financiers.
                 Sidney hated the glib tone of newspapers.
   His scruples were incorrigible.

I wanted to ask him what it all mattered.
   Bernard Baruch would never visit

His stuffy, overheated classroom. Instead I listened
   and thought at times I heard inside Sidney's

Clockwork rants about who got noticed in this
   money-hungry world and who didn't

And who read Herodotus and Plutarch
   and who knew them only as names,

Something more frightfully prideful
than either wealth or hurt.

Kid

It's easy to be possessive about
Predilections. Breathing, for instance.
It stays the same, asks no favors,
Yet grows and grows, fomenting

So many dear and prosaic attachments.
I have to have this, I say but
Then forget what *this* is yet refuse
To be embarrassed the next time desire

Spreads its sticky wings. It's hard
To sit on the top step of the back porch
Or in the rocking chair by the wood fire
And think about nothing, just be a body

Without the slimmest sense of ownership, letting
Evening be evening. It seems inhuman
To let anything float, not to rile the surface,
Challenge the depths, comment liberally

In the face of crepuscular indifference.
Words stream out like bees on a summer morning.
They vanish and more appear.
What are you getting at, kid? my Grandpa

Izzy used to say when I went on and on
About my earnest, textured perceptions.
I looked into his yellow, rheumy eyes.
Oh, Grandpa, can this habit ever mend?

Vaudeville

Two bubbles sat in a basin
At the beginning
Of the twentieth century
And one bubble said to the other,
"Hours minutes seconds."
The other said, "What do you think
About Teddy Roosevelt, Oscar
Wilde, the discovery of radium?"
Downstairs the maid closed

A pantry door and dabbed at
Her eyes with a worn handkerchief.
Her suitor, one Robert Emmett Sweeney,
Was going back to the old country.
America was an absence of feeling,
He had told her last evening.
Cleopatra, the house cat,
Yawned in the thick, afternoon sun.

The first bubble said that
Wilde got what he deserved.
He'd believed that wit was holy.
"Hours minutes seconds,"
The other bubble trilled.
The maid began to prepare dinner
Opening and shutting drawers angrily.
Thin vibrations made their way
Through the balloon frame house
Though the bubbles, those knights
Of brisk frailty, had more to say.

(for Jeanne Marie Beaumont)

Meditating (New England, 1892)

Fog, wind, rocks, fir trees—
The blank face of eternity indifferently burns.
Two men, one young, one middle-aged,
Sit Japanese style, meditating,
Staring out at the North Atlantic.

The June sunrise is joy exploding
And gilding the steel water.
There is no big explosion yet.
It is toward the end of the nineteenth century,
The proper century, and the men,
Who are wealthy and idle, are worried
And ill at ease.

The umbrageous gulls shrill mercilessly.
A crab dawdles by the two gentlemen.
Waves slap and slam and slither.
The men hear and see and sniff
The salt, agnostic air.

They are men of uncommon attainments,
Tutors and tutees,
Connoisseurs of languages, boats, prints,
Glazes, cloudless June days—
And yet there is nothing to attain.

Water runs over rocks
And falls back into itself.
Spray hovers, sparkles, and dissolves
In one unaccented second.
Sand trickles through fine fingers.

They sit and look at the sea
And conjure up other centuries
And other men who walked more
Purposefully through crueler worlds,
Who orated and argued and thieved.

They hike for hours over boulders and
Through thick spruce woods.
As Yankees, they are too habitually
Vigorous to be truly effete.
It's rather that the iron in their souls is slag
Because they suspect they have no souls
And are no more than waves, the groping
And tumult and final lassitude
Of some happenstance of energy.
They are arbitrary.

It will be a good year for blueberries.
Morning after morning the sky shouts with light.
The two men sit precisely as
They were instructed in the city of Kyoto
And as they have read in certain rare books.

"Whatever are you doing, George?"
A mother on a veranda asks impatiently

And her son, a handsome man for whom
Cities were built and fortunes lodged,
Only smiles faintly, says nothing, and,
With his hands pressed together, bows.

For Jane Kenyon

So tempting to imagine the unindustrious
Perfection of her future.
Any string of loose-fitting days would
Have done, any sequence
Of fate's cards but that one.

Poems are like cats: they sit and
Loll and stretch and then
They pounce with terrible precision.
Blood feathers hair
And tiny, ever-so-brief cries.

Some days it seems odd that
The poems should need days.
They exist so serenely, even their pains
Are serene—not stoic but
Delicately throbbing like phlox fingered

By October's first frost.
Always flowers raising their gainly heads.
"Appreciate what you have,"
Many of us were told as children.
Your poems are the monstrance. We try.

Melancholy Baby

(In memoriam, W.M.)

You sit at the end of the bar
Beneath the basketball game
On the TV. The people look at you
Partially, which suits your permanent mood.
Though it's a different bar tonight
You order the usual. Contemplating too long tends to
Bring on a triple shot of trouble.
Something exciting has happened in the game;
There's a briefly fervent look in people's eyes.
You peer into your drink. It's no Sargasso Sea
And you're no diver. There's something akin to joy
In being so world-weary.

You walk into the funeral home
And announce yourself as a business
Associate because we all are business
Associates in America even if
We high-mindedly try to ignore it or join
A transcendent cult or just blisslessly screw up
On what seems like our own.
The fact is for so punctilious a presence
Time has some pretty irregular habits
Like someone who has a lot of old
Dry cleaning slips in the bottom of her purse.
Where is that beige wool coat?
Time doesn't return any calls, then pulls
The phone from the wall jack, hurls it through
A closed window, and stomps out of the apartment
Muttering, "It's forever, you flesh-and-blood fucker, it's forever."
Grief wants some air freshener.
The coffin glows like an old-moneyed smile.

You sit down on a folding chair in the last row
At the poetry reading. A man is decanting
His ironic ambitions. A woman is throwing exquisite
Knives at her hapless childhood. It's not so much
Enlightening as recklessly appalling.
You can respect that.
The art of diceyness lays some rigorous odds.
Afterward the patter starts up again
Like an election campaign or machine
But how else could it be?

You lie awake and polish some words.
You never know when you might want one of them.
In your blue eyes there are no reprobates.
All moments are pickled in this
Ingenuous, articulate brine.
It's neither reassuring nor unkind.
Everything will be open again in the morning.
You might sleep sometime.

Son (1957)

Hot Sunday mornings he'd be there
On the back porch dressed rather neatly
For someone not going anywhere.
He swore by the virtues of seersucker;
His shoes were thick with polish.
He was never what they used to call a "bum."
He'd be drinking whiskey and beer
Deliberately, intently, methodically.

Words are the ashes of feelings
Some dour Englishmen once said.
I had the hardest time to say, "Hi, Dad"
As I walked around him to get to
The plentiful newspaper. What had
Duke Snider done and Stan Musial?
My heroes, they were always in it.
There was an empty lot across the alleyway,

Patches of chicory and mullein growing there—
The flowers that nobody wants.
Not that it bothered them or me
For that matter as I settled back into
The plastic comfort of a lightweight lawn chair
And resolved to first read the world news
Of speeches and guns while my father
Said nothing. Liquid gushed and glass clinked.

Bobbin'

"If I find out that she's been bobbin'
On his knob, I'll kill her," the lady in
Front of me on the Liberty Heights Avenue bus
Confided to the lady beside her who continued
To knit something pink. I, the seventeen-year-old
Virgin behind them, wanted to ask her if her
Daughter could do some bobbin' with my knob
That had only encountered the sparseness
Of air thus far—want being the mantra of the shy
Who are doomed to overestimate everything,
Whose awkwardness is raw, minute, and relentless.
I wanted to throw away my damn textbooks.
Geometry! No wonder there was rock 'n' roll for
The quivering likes of me. How did I keep my food down?
My hidden feeling was one more puerile agony.
"Help me!" I wanted to shout though not to the lady
With the daughter as she launched into a summary
Of the outrageous calumnies she'd endured from her
"Own flesh and blood." Various girl-women got on
The bus and I uncraftily eyed each one.
They tittered, looked out windows, studied.
One put a tiny radio up to her perfect ear.
Need is the genius of love, I might have had
Embroidered on the back of my school jacket
Below my letter for playing in the band.
The lady rose at Gwynn Oak Drive, did not
Look back at me as her form staggered forward.
She too, once, I thought. *And more than once.*

January

"Cold as the moon," he'd mutter
In the January of 5 A.M. and 15 below
As he tried to tease the old Chev into greeting
One more misanthropic morning.

It was an art (though he never
Used that curious word) as he thumped
The gas pedal and turned the key
So carefully while he held his breath
And waited for the sharp jounce
And roar of an engaged engine.

"Shoulda brought in the battery last night."
"Shoulda got up around midnight
And turned it over once."

It was always early rising as he'd worked
A lifetime "in every damn sort
Of damn factory." Machines were
As natural to him as dogs and flowers.
A machine, as he put it, "was sensible."

I was so stupid about valves and intakes
He thought I was some religious type.
How had I lived as long as I had
And remained so out of it?
And why had I moved of my own free will
To a place that prided itself
On the blunt misery of January?

"No way to live," he'd say as he poked
A finger into the frozen throat

Of an unwilling carburetor.
His breath hung in the air
Like a white balloon.

Later on the way to the town where
We worked while the heater
Wheezed fitfully and the windshield
Showed indifference to the defroster
He'd turn to me and say that
The two best things in this world
Were hot coffee and winter sunrises.
The icy road beckoned to no one,
Snow began to drift down sleepily,
The peace of servitude sighed and dreamed.

An Academic Family in the 50s

Blue teakettle boiling petulantly,
Scraps of British centuries handed down
Lovingly though hard by now to identify,
The quotes evoked more for Anglo effect than content.

Contempt
For the nascent mush of television:
"Yet another chapter in the already bulging annals
Of human idiocy.

God save us from anything that glows."
"And what is the good of that," the eldest child
Inquired calmly, "your dislikings?
I like things—

Chocolate Easter bunnies, for instance, and Superman.
Are you as helpful as Superman?"
To which a husband and father would insist
Through the glow of aged whiskey

That good works were beside the point.
The existential quick was his domain
Though he strayed in a Hemingway way.
"There was once a woman," a wife and mother

Explained, "who was not Emma Bovary."
"Jump down a well, chew on a brick,"
A blond child caroled.
"Keep up your belt, don't touch your dick."

In the small hours of the calm night
A voice arose from a third floor

Bedroom calling out
Piteously

For the succoring arms of daylight.
Snores, faint rustlings, the electric
Vigilance of hall lights. Dream-silence.
The June morning was serene, coolly sunny,

The wind through the screen doors
A soft, green chant.
On the breakfast table, half-read were
Camus, A.A. Milne, *The Pride of the Yankees*,

A paperback of crossword puzzles,
The Hardy Boys, James Joyce, and Agatha Christie.
"I know," everyone is saying at once
To one another and the word-riddled universe.

(for Kate Barnes)

Satan Reviews the Cuban Missile Crisis

Not yet . . . and yet there remains a wealth
Of hours and minutes and all other manner of
Lowly human enumerations and yet so near . . .

To see the boy president and the fat Russian
Toss the ball of life back and forth,
Each one juggling like a clown yet so grave-
Faced was such splendidly apocalyptic fun.

If it was not at last the stuff of well-
Deserved destruction, their callow principles
Blown not sky-high but hell-deep, still it
Was lively enough to give an admittedly jaded
Retiree a chance to stand before his full-
Length mirror and practice a speech or two—
Not so much of seduction or canny desperation
As pragmatism, that malleable common sense
That came in after the rash and surly Milton
(A prince too in his regicide way I'm glad to grant).

Who would believe at this point in what fallen humans
Call "time," that objectivity could be the prime mover of grief,
Pain, and discontent on such a scale that
No preening, hotheaded, smoke-blowing lieutenant of mine
Could grasp the devastation dispassion has
Improvised?
                Ah foresight, that fable of theologues,
How I wish that a glimmer of human ignorance
Might rise for just one morning and scorch
The Lord's handiwork to black crumbs.

Still, if there was not so much divine
Intervention in this case (as if there ever was),
The reasons that made the Reds (I like that word)
Pull back and the skirt-chasing,
Cardboard militarist Jack Kennedy show
Himself to be more temperate than wily were
The usual patchworks·of face-saving folderol.

I know—I've had advisors of my own filling my ears
With the gas of their brilliant egos.

I've been there and done that and when
I look "years later" (as they innocently put it)
On the same morose inclinations and missiles
I see cause for me to rejoice.
                                        I've licked
My wounds till my spittle is honey and I do
Not feel sorry for those fools.
                                        Ever.

Spirits of the Mall

The ghosts of south Florida gather at
A mall north of Miami. They hang,
As a few of them wryly put it, mostly
They look and exclaim about the new models.
Some died before there were microwaves
And CDs and personal computers and
They have to pester the more recently dead
As to what those things are called and what they do.
Still, there are always refrigerators and TVs
To sigh over—"so big," "so wide," "so clear
And clean."
                    The young people in the malls
With their baseball caps worn backward and various
Earrings do not recognize the presence of
The spirit world. After all it is air-conditioned
And their own bodies are so beguilingly taut.
Who could know that the recirculated air is speaking?
It isn't on their wavelength and they
Laugh and scowl and preen for their secret loves.
For the ghosts' part they stick to the machines.
Old machines get made into new ones
Or they sit peacefully in dumps and woods
And swamps changing very little from day to day.
New machines are promises that come true.
Being human was a phase.
                              At three in the morning
Only the workers from Central America are there
Mopping and vacuuming. Some of the spirits
Want to help but no one likes to be tapped
On the shoulder by a ghost. These people, though,
May be more likely to believe. They too pause
And look in the windows and stare and comment

42

About camcorders, floor models, rebates,
4-head VCRs, phones, though they can care
Only in that human way—so fickle, so unaware.

Barmaid

You start looking into people's eyes—
A flat but friendly stare
Right into them—and you want
To stop looking into people's eyes
Because you can't help but see—
We're helpless that way—and it's
Not secrets or some kind of romancing
Bullshit that schoolgirls want
To believe in but this drop, this
Giddy drop like a ride at the fun park,
That throws your stomach over because
You see how solitary it is in there
And if that sounds sappy because
A bunch of these people are categorically
No good—husband beaters, wife beaters,
Kid beaters, dog beaters—you don't
Understand why they're drinking in the first
Place, which is to take a little bit of
The curse off for a little while so that
Their eyes expand into blank pools
And the anger of fragility goes away
Until tomorrow when I look again
And I see the soul's animal light
In their mostly ugly faces and I see
My face in the mirror across the room
Like the woman in the painting by a man
Named Edward Manet who looks
Very straightforwardly and almost dully
Into space and you can feel all she's
Taken in, some nobody like me, not
A history book sort of person, and you
Can feel that if she ever smiles

It's for the pleasure of distraction,
Of the overheard and passing by
Because it makes her eyes forget
The sad wealth inside each moment.

Explication du Texte

One midwinter night in the tacky
But cozy grad club after a beer
Or two and the usual chat about
Our overbearing, neurotic profs
You emerged from a musing silence
To announce that as a lapsed Catholic
The only heaven for which you could muster
Any fervor was Wallace Stevens's:
"Consider (you said), it is piquant
Yet amiable, voluble yet courtly.
Delirious with chatter
And bewildered grace. What
(You asked) was the Christian heaven but
An insipid smile, an anaesthetic
That Stevens cheerily challenged,
Fashioning his own cock's crow of sublimity
From his proudly pagan taste.
The best of heavens is implied in
The imagination's zest. Unblessed it is blessed."

I felt far away from any heaven
In that sealed tomb of cigarettes
And denimed *philosophes* though
That didn't keep me from skewering
The insurance-man poet as being "in reality"
(A favorite, all-purpose, idiot phrase
Of mine) an armchair fascist and fantasist,
A cold-blooded Prospero who summoned
Elegancies because he couldn't abide
The contingent pain of mere flesh.
His heaven was the leisure class's wallpaper.

"Don't give me that pissed-off, working-class jive,"
You said, looking aggrieved and bleary at the same time.
"Stevens despised the wisdom of wariness.
The man sang joy from the grayest air."

I wouldn't bend. Frost held me that
Year like an instructive nightmare.
His shrewd gravity was my longed-for
Compass. We fenced half-heartedly,
Downed our Buds, eyed the clock
Donated by a local realtor for the minute
To repair to our bookish cells.
Awkward hurt spoke in your gentle eyes.
When on earth would our words have lives?

Les Demoiselles

I walk in the bank to deposit
A pension check first thing in
The morning and the tellers are all

Fresh and made-up with that care
I have always marveled at and they are
Standing there waiting and

I choose Cindy who smiles
Completely, a flower-in-midsummer smile,
Full of light and youth and as much

Joy as could be in a brick building
And I think back to a brothel I
Used to go to in France right after

The war. It's not a wicked thought
And not because I'm old and it's all
A memory anyway but because I remember

The sight of those women in a more-
Or-less row and their looking at me
With amiable contempt, feigned longing,

And unfeigned worldliness. I was a man,
They were women, that was the end of it.
I say "Good morning" to her smile

And I can feel her voice take on a calm
Pleasure as if she's looking into what once
Was there and wondering and looking

Again at the shuffling old-guy presenting
His check and hearing in his voice
The echo of a long-standing sentiment.

Fatality

I was in the store buying the usual—
Coffee, gas, the paper—when I heard
Sonny Parlin's voice on the scanner that
Dave Massenger had barricaded himself
In his house and there were staties everywhere.

Some nightmares you dream in advance and then
You walk into them and they play themselves out
To the last card in the inexorable deck.
Dave started shooting and a marksman (who was
Also a 'Nam vet) drilled him. One shot in the head.

It was front page the next day and the day after
It was a tractor-trailer tipping over on
The interstate and the day after that a guy
Shot his ex-wife in the parking lot outside
Kmart and after that I lost track.

It was weeks before I went over to see
His wife, Maria. She was sitting in the kitchen
Drinking a cup of herbal tea. The leaves
Were all gone off the trees and the sky was that
Autumnal electric blue and the wind was blowing

Hard and fresh out of Canada. "He saw a lot
Of wicked shit," she said. "He'd visited hell
But he'd put it behind him. I mean he was living
With life, putting one foot in front of the other,
Not trying too hard to be too good."

My eyes strayed around the room and wound
Up resting on a high school picture that had to

Have been Dave, one of those goggle-eyed
Pictures from the senior yearbook. He was
In-country not more than a year later.

Maria started talking about their trip
To Disney World and how Dave had gone
Up to Mickey Mouse and given him a big
Fat kiss. We laughed, then felt the silence.
It was going to start snowing soon.

A Benediction (Homage to Marguerite Yourcenar)

The master told Akiba the slave that he, Akiba,
   must lie with the master's wife, Ramona.
The master watched them perform this congress;
   he did not wish to be deceived.
He himself had grown weary of women's watery charms.
Akiba groaned, Ramona made a low whistling sound.
She conceived a son whom the master named David.

A few years later Akiba was sold to a merchant
   from Venice.
The master placed his hands on Akiba's shoulders
   the night before the slave departed.
   He gave him a small calfskin pouch.
Ramona watched the slave walk down the road
   beside a donkey
   until there was only dust and light.

On the ship voyage a vicious storm came up.
Within sight of the island of Cyprus the vessel foundered.
Three men made it to the island and one of them,
   gasping with terror and hope, was Akiba the slave.

There he lived, neither free nor unfree, an alien
   who came to be an expert tanner in whose hands
   stiff hides became as soft as baby's skin.
On many evenings he sat beneath a shade tree
   and sang in a droning voice to anyone who cared to hear
   a few songs about fate that were of immemorial provenance.

One day Akiba saw a young man in the marketplace.
The man wasn't buying, merely inquiring and looking.

52

How could he tell, how could he know
    if this man was his son?
It was a feeling Akiba had, a feeling attached
    to a person who walked with long, graceful strides.
He ran after the young man but when he looked
    into the stranger's face he saw nothing,
    only a sunburnt, surprised squint.

That night Akiba went to the shore
    and after saying a benediction threw a coin
    of recent derivation into the dark, calm sea.

Poem for My Son

Each time you connected I strode among junipers
And ankle-twisting stump-holes to where it seemed the ball
　　had landed.
You waited and gave occasional directions:
"In front of the apple tree. To the right of the boulder, I think."
Before each pitch arrived your boy's body grew taut.
You were like a green snake—lithe, patient, concentrated.

In spring, the hardball's plummet
Ended in a soggy plop. Grounders skidded rather than bounced.
In summer there were wild strawberries—
The tiniest winces of fruit sugar.
We lolled in the modest northern heat and watched
The grasshoppers inherit the earth.

Sometimes while throwing the ball I critiqued
Your swing: "The most difficult of physical feats,
Hitting a baseball. "Or I chattered: "The game was not invented
In America but evolved like a—"
You were correct to interrupt. Pleasure wanted
The uncanny knack of concentration: not bearing down too hard
Nor assuming valiant strength would right all flaws.

You rarely flailed in vain. Eventually, you could have
Started for any school team, but we lived far away
From the practiced accuracy of diamonds.
Whatever was to be learned, in all its green amplitude,
Had to be done there, on a sloping, runneled field.

Draft Morning (1969)

I'd been taking low-dosage downers for a couple of years—
Not to the point of being melodramatically
Addicted but not able to look life in the face
Without the helpful hand of pharmacology either.
And I'd been talking to a shrink who kept
An unlit cigar in his mouth and went to Wellfleet
For a month in the summer and who nodded
Occasionally as I babbled and even less
Occasionally asked me a question—"When did
That happen, Baron?" or "Who said that to you?"—
That upon later reflection seemed so mundane
As to make my stomach churn with grief.

A mellow hell, my mother dying of cancer in bits
And pieces, lying in a hospital bed, her eyes
Unfocused, her spirit buried beneath painkillers
So that she seemed an ethereal zombie or a super-
Annuated piece of machinery, a relic of a purpose.
And the war that followed you into the grocery store
Checkout aisle so that when I looked up from the jars
Of gefilte fish for my grandmother and the newest
Sugar-dosed cereals for my younger sisters,
There were the newsmagazines with photos of leaders,
Helicopters, and increasingly, snapshots from their
High school yearbooks of guys who'd been blown away.
We knew, of course, what we were doing. That's what
The living have the right to say although I wasn't much
Of a true believer and one day when I picked up my
Dodge Dart at the garage where I'd gotten the brake
Shoes replaced, Joe Flaherty, the family mechanic whom
I'd known since childhood asked me how I was doing
And in response, out of the exasperated blue, I said

"The war bites it" and he walked around the counter
And put his face directly up to mine and told me
I was a poor excuse for an American,
That brave men were dying in that jungle this minute
While I spouted my two-bit opinions. I thought
There was more sadness in his voice than rage.

So when one cool and celestially clear autumn
Morning I walked into a downtown building that seemed
Like a cross between an old hotel and an armory,
I wasn't afraid or confident but numb and zoned out.
There was instant camaraderie and instant wariness
And most of all a lot of scoffing among the guys
In the endless lines because that's really all
A nineteen-year-old can do is scoff at the quiet weight
On his tender shoulders, scoffing at death and the army
And girlfriends and parents and other guys, scoffing
At everything. So when I looked in the eyes of the bored
And harassed army shrink, I knew I was at one
Of those bridges that takes you somewhere you didn't know
About or even want to know about if you were willing
To step out of line and be half-honest with yourself.
I told him I couldn't do it, and he said in a voice
Just like his eyes, "Is that so, son? Is that so?"
And wrote something down on a carbon paper form and
Blurted out "next" as he motioned me away from
His uncluttered desk.
                        Three blocks away in the pale
Late-afternoon light I threw a vial of pills
Into the gutter—a self-conscious, self-loathing gesture—
And I sat a long time at the steering wheel, not

Turning the key, quivering like some bug
In its inordinate flight.

Acting Out

If inappropriateness was the unwanted genius
 Of the scarifying sixties, the sacrifice of modest,
Melting pot cohesion for the passion of
 The unmoored moment, then my acned, "it's-a-sign-
Of-virility" friend John Hanscomb was an arbiter,
 Avatar, and aviator of experiences so purposefully
Edgy that falling off third-story balconies
 Seemed a relief compared to the confrontations
That were for John the routinely hair-raising
 Hoodoo that made the drabness of our similar
Physical and mental equipment somewhat tolerable
 As when he went into a honky-tonk in south
Baltimore and proceeded to rail in an increasingly
 Southern-Comfort-soaked voice about the ungodly puling
Whininess of country western music. At first
 People showed very faint smiles but as John
Pushed his rant further (harpooning icons like
 Patsy Cline) I could feel the ugliness condense
Like snow clouds and it was only the ministering
 Angel of a bartender who said, "The door's over
There, kid," and pulled out some humongous
 Smith-and-Wesson-type revolver which he aimed
At John's person that saved us from another
 Emergency room sit-in.
                                Or when John would put
On his astronaut suit (right down to the bubble helmet)
 And go to the bank to cash a check and make
Small talk about how degraded life on earth was becoming,
 How we Americans were awfully lucky to be
Exploring space because *this* planet was going
 To be history "pretty darn soon" as he tried to
Expressively snap his heavily gloved fingers.

His accent was Midwestern techno-geek,
Down-home with an interstellar echo.

Not far down the path into the disco woods of
The seventies John met heroin and lost among
   Other things his socially unsocial sense of humor.
You couldn't even say he died young since he was
   A "half-assed ancient" as he once put it.
We'd get stoned and read *The Narrow Road to the Deep North*
   And talk about how Basho was on such friendly
Terms with bugs and mud. We pictured ourselves
   Tramping America's byways and writing haiku
That we posted on town bulletin boards beside papers
   About fishing licenses and AA meetings.

That the road doesn't go
   On forever, that it barely goes over the next hill,
Doesn't take away from how John lived for those times
   When people's eyes started to yeast with startled
Incomprehension and they looked hard at him as if
   To make sure he was there in front of them and not
Somehow elsewhere. I think he loved them then—
   Not their confusion but their coiled souls, their spark.

Jack, Age 23, in Canada (1972)

"I'm here on a courtesy call.
I'm here on a coward's errand.
I'm here because I like winter.
I'm here because in eighth grade I saw
    Tom Wheeler beat Joey Simpson to a whimpering pulp
    and didn't try to break it up.
I'm here because Jesus has nothing
    against Asians.
I'm here because my father kicked me out.
I'm here because I wanted to handle
    some different money.
I'm here as my own ambassador.
I'm here because I don't believe in empires.
I'm here because my flesh is infested
    with feelings.
I'm here on a nation call."

While washing dishes in a Chinese
Restaurant in Toronto he sought to perfect
The Bob Hope smile—
That pinched essence of self-promotion,
Golf course confidence, and cozy wit.
He mounted a small mirror above the sink
And worked at it till his mouth ached.
His employers were (he wrote in a letter)
"Amused in their taciturn way."

A conscientious surrealist, he spent his spare time
Trying to pry open literature's most baffled doors.
Kafka and Beckett and Dostoyevsky
    all pleased him breathlessly
As if they were debutantes at a cotillion.

Absurdity was the faith of his disbelief;
His agony was okay.

His high school yearbook was his crucible
As he noted whether the smiling face forgave him:
Three girls and a guy out of one-
    hundred-twenty-nine.

"Spare me the empathetic sensitivities,"
He used to bark to me over the halting
Phone connection.

I protested but finally complied.

A tarnished, cloud-scudding November morning
Brings back some long gone sense of him:
His ardent slouch; his impatience with
    the pretensions of eastern colleges;
The delicate fingers rolling perfect cigarettes;
His praise of cats, jazz trumpet, the passionate
    suspense of chess.

I can see his brown eyes,
Furious and so unhappily pure.

Route One-Thirty

Empty as the apartment to which she drives home
And frank as death, the winter evening falls
Calmly over Route One-Thirty.
The car spins measurably and the few
French fries left over from her drive-thru lunch
Smell nasty. Were they food?
Would ants treasure them? She winces at
The outside air that touches her through a bit
Of window she has left healthily open.
The air almost arctic tonight yet

The road is so cheerful, so superbly lit.
The river of cars flows so peacefully
As if in thematic concert.
Above the neon signs darkness begins
And that is comforting too somehow,
The finality of it, the limited range
Of the most emphatic human signs—
Eat Here, Buy This, See That.
Look a few feet higher up in the air
And all claims have vanished. She's between

Marriages or above the self-satisfaction of love
Or bemused to the point of crying (later) into
Her microwaved soup. Now she is driving
And the air is cold and the sky black
And she sings to herself a song
From childhood about a spellbound princess,
For she is tired from her work
And accountably sad and surprised
That even tonight in her six-cylinder skull
Nothing wants banishing or getting right.

Family Affairs

She'd been in Chicago on business
So she heard about it days later
That Aunt Simmie had died.
She sent a card for which

She was rebuked on the phone
By her late mother's brother, Harold,
"Cards? Cards are for lazy people.
Our tears must water the earth."

She took Harold and Marilyn
For Chinese. "Why do you work so hard?
Harold has a heart condition.
Do you date Gentiles? They're murderers."

The firm got a new account in Pittsburgh
And it meant traveling twice a month.
One night she got home from
The jetport and put on the answering

Machine to hear her cousin Esther's
Bewildered voice: "Harold's had it."
She'd missed the funeral by a day.
She lay in bed and wondered

About his last eloquent words.
Morning offered the softest blue sky
And a paper in which people died
Like insects. An Arab woman, her face

Dazed with grief, stared at her
From page three. The phone was silent.

She felt the pulse in her neck
As if blood were testimony.

Portrait of the Artist

I woke in the bitter, dark, winter morning.
I was eight.

There were the smells of the cat who slept
In my room on a braided rug, of eggs being fried

In the kitchen down the hall, of flannel pajamas,
Of the apartment's mahogany air.

There was dressing and then there was school.
I had hands but lacked the capable motions.

I staggered and stuttered, unkempt as a mongrel.
I dreaded putting on the one light in my little room,

A table lamp shaped like an old, New York City skyscraper.
Light was so nasty.

There was the blue smell of cold metal pipes.
I had to get up.

Why didn't familiarity make anything easier?
Putting my socks on, combing my hair, deciding

Which of my three pairs of identical shoes I should wear....
I held my hands in front of me

Like some sort of faith healer.
I looked at the little mezzotint on the wall of Christ.

He was so sweet and baleful.
He was so little help to me.

Winter was a cap your mother had knit that you
Didn't want to wear because it was unmanly.

Winter was a grudge.
Winter was the silent type like Brother James

Who never spoke when he thrashed you.
I went to the window and breathed upon it

And traced my initials in the beautiful steam.
My father called. My day was done.

O Mother Europe (1931)

The milky smell of indecision clung to
Their clothes and gestures and words.
Hope lisped softly, an incredulous

Servant who did not believe what she had heard.
O Mother Europe, had civilization's oration ended?
Had the God of cathedrals forgotten that

The Jews were the original moral headline,
The answer to aimless darkness? Or was God Europe?
Had He become the punctuating trains,

The shirt collars, plumbing, the clamorous phone?
People chatted gaily about their lives
As if the fates had retired.

Perhaps everyone now was a Jew or no one.
On the avenues ideas threw stones and eggs,
In estimable parlors études shivered,

Bravado screamed for the healthy rain of death.
The milky smell of indecision hung in the violet air,
Yielding and taut and slim as spiders' webs,

Hung above leaf-strewn paths and glass storefronts.
The milky caution of gentleness lay down
In the gutter and muttered like the torpor of belief.

Furniture

The Abramowitz brothers had
A furniture store downtown.
They were cousins on my mother's side
Of the family and unlike everyone else
I knew who was in retail (and it
Seemed as though everyone was)
They didn't complain about their
Customers in tones of Biblical affliction.
In fact when someone said what has
Become termed the *n* word, one or
The other of them would say in
An earnest yet snitty voice
That their customers were colored people
And good decent people who worked
Hard for their money and knew a good value.

The brothers didn't live in the suburbs;
They lived in brick houses in a semi-
Gentrified neighborhood a couple of miles
From the store and they gave parties attended
By people from both races who actually
Talked to each other and drank
The same liquor from the same paper cups.

I remember wandering around in the store,
Plopping myself down on mattresses, swiveling
Padded lounge chairs, gazing at dining room groupings
That looked like sets from a daytime
Television series. The brothers loved
Furniture. They'd run a hand over a tabletop
The way a trainer would touch a thoroughbred.
Furniture was in their blood.

One night the older brother Lenny was shot
To death behind the store. The kid who
Popped him got twenty-five dollars from
Lenny's wallet. Al sold out
And moved to California.

The store burnt down a few years later.
In retrospect the brothers were denounced
By the local African-American press as little
Better than loan sharks. They were trying
To make a buck, my mother would sigh.

In dreams, dining room tables beckon to me.
I see the endless row houses of Baltimore and
Patient hands polishing cherrywood, maple,
Oak, mahogany, ash. This isn't some
Pressed-together plywood, Lenny would say.
This is a tree, madam, this is a tree.

Bullshit and truth, colored and white,
Yes and no. He died, my mother said,
For what he believed.

News

Staring at the suavely haggard visages
Of the news commentators of the long ago 50s,
My grandmother would opine that no one loved
The news better than Moskowitz, a neighbor
Of hers, in the longer ago 30s.

His face had glowed like a radio dial (she said)
With information he needed to impart:
How the landlord was seen exiting a divorcee's
Apartment at three in the morning
Or how Stalin was going to make up with Trotsky

Or how the New York Giants baseball team
Had signed a Negro player. Lies, half-truths,
Nuclei of facts, confusions, libels, deprecations—
I could picture the informer, a nervous
Little man sitting down to a cup of vigorous tea

In my grandparents' kitchen and declaiming
What he had heard or seen or read or imagined.
With God there is no news, my grandmother offered
By way of shrugging, take-it-or-leave-it
Explanation. I chewed on that one while Walter

Cronkite looked ever more serious, his voice
A resonant seismograph of world crises.
How could we avoid our febrile natures?
We were, after all, creations, lesser things
Whose seats were farther away from

The primal stage in both time and space.
Our own deaths seemed like rumors despite

A wealth of stern evidence. I chewed
And remembered that according to my grandma
Moskowitz was a man who disappeared. Vanished.

The paper was on his doorsill; his clothes
Lay folded in his bureau. There was a quart of milk
In the icebox and some noodle pudding.
"His news ran out," Grandma said and,
As was her less-than-scrupulous habit, laughed.

The Great Depression

The glow of pennies in a quart canning jar
The glow of the numinous wooden radio
The glow of late May...
It was as if a giant had swallowed an era whole

And all the people and trees and buildings
And dogs and cats
Lived there in his stomach.
It was as if time were a parent

Placing a permanent hand on your shoulder....
Definition is a horizon
Even dreams must obey as
They exalt on another plane the burnished day.

Banks moaned and armies rattled
And the fireflies came out and the snow fell
As children lay patiently in their beds
Waiting to be told a story that sweetly murdered time....

Once there was a little man with a mustache
Who could roar like an aeroplane.
He lived in a topsy-turvy house on a dismal street
Beside a canal full of oak leaves....

In the middle of the confining night
The nexus of human nerves awakens
And lies there worried yet
Cozy as a coin in a rich man's pocket.

Outside on the street or prairie
There is no outside....

The giant relaxes and sings a polka-like song
About a little man with a mustache

Who stamps his feet on the speaker's platform
Like an angry pony. . . .
There are cheers like fields of wheat,
Then everyone sleeps.

For the Yiddish Poets

Poof poof poof! Languages people cities
Gone in the breadth of a cat's whisker,
Gone in a tyrant's belch,
Gone in a terse good-night.
I blinked one morning while getting out of bed and
A phrase I had honed for three insomniac hours
Vanished. Where is the tissue paper of eternity
That might wrap our hapless largesse?

Poof poof poof!
I sneezed on the el and my droplets dispersed
Among the throng of grunting, shaky humanity.
In two weeks a fever fells a butcher in the Bronx.
"Never been sick a day in his murderous life":
His wife swears it over coffee to
A neighbor who shakes her head and mumbles a prayer.

Poof poof poof!
Typhoid Annie was a Jew, one of the prophets
Who is awaiting entry into the latter-day Torah,
One of the festering saints who polished
Misfortune till it glowed like a malignant ruby.

Poof poof poof!
My huzzahs have a Fourth-of-July, *goyishe*,
Patriotic, *shikse*-loving ring to them.
My tongue hungers for blueberry pie, ballpark hot dogs,
The tangy, cloying fizz of a slightly warm cola.
My tongue greets English with the vociferous
Friendliness of a vote-cadging alderman. I favor
Mongrel languages spoken by demonstrative recalcitrants.

Poof poof poof!
I spill a little coffee on the counter of a restaurant
On Second Avenue and within seconds a waitress
Smiles at my idiocy and wipes the surface clean
With a damp cloth she can twirl like a rope.
What might emerge from those drops? They disappear no more
Than the souls of our forebears disappeared, than our tears
In Egypt disappeared, than our house in the Pale of Settlement
That was torched in a pogrom disappeared. Are you acquainted
With ashes? They rise in the air but then they settle
On the earth, they are underfoot this very moment.
They are speaking to one another. Whether you know
Their language or not is immaterial. They know yours.

Poof poof poof!
Sorrow dissolves in the chicken fat of daylight, the horns of
The taxicabs, a fat old guy standing on a street corner puffing
On a cigar, a poet clairvoyant with passion thrusting a piece of
Paper into a friend's hand. Read this read this read this!

Christmas

The quietest day. Even when we spoke in
Ordinary tones to say we wanted jam not butter
On our toast, it sounded muffled and distant.
We stayed inside and avoided each other,

Not from dislike but wariness, as if
Our guarded faces might dissolve and confess.
We must have read a lot—Dickens for
My mother, military history for Dad,

Adventures and fantasies for us kids.
I always seemed to be reading Jack London.
Now and then, I'd look up from my book and listen.
What did I want to hear? Exclamations,

Carols, prayers, supernal sleighs? And my own voice,
Certain yet misbegotten, chosen yet left out?

A Roman

Lately Gaius Claudius
Has grown weary of his dreams.
It isn't the tedium of adulteries
Or the malice of murder that disturbs him;
It's the pettiness and multitude of his desires,
How they insert themselves into every nook
Of his nocturnal mind, forcing him in ardent,
Unflinching detail to betray secrets, steal coins,
Fib for no reason, drink beyond satiation.

A victim of his itinerant sensations, he can see
The Christians differently, their pallor and
Their fierceness and he hates that unwanted wisdom.
A body of iron with handsome wounds
From many campaigns and a mind as
Soft as a sheep's guts. How?

He rises in the morning haggard and unfit.
He walks through the city that
Made him a man, saluting his equals,
Knowing that they see the signs of his distress.
When he finds himself by the river,
He thinks of those sad notions the Christians have,
Of their all-seeing god and their
Faith in the strength of unsanctioned rites.

The sun glances playfully off the calm river.
He lowers his head as in an obeisance,
As if to heal what he cannot protect.

Homage to J.D. Salinger

Coming home from away basketball games
In the dead January upstate night,
With nothing to look at for that hour or two
Beside signs for towns we'd never go to,
Living rooms awash in

The blue glow of television, liquor stores,
Laundromats, cornfields lost under dunes of snow,
We'd play this game called "End of the World."
We'd sit there in the dark, each guy on his own
Bus seat and come up with possibilities that ranged

From "We'll fry the sky" or "The roaches will rule"
To "Mr. Spencer, the school principal,
Will suspend the universe for cosmic insolence."
It was weird—what was there in our minds
And how we could say it only on a bus ride.

One night Goggles Lapchik got real serious in his voice
As if he were going to give a talk at the annual banquet
About how we all pulled together as a team this year
And sacrificed our egos and then he cut a fart
To blow a door off its hinges. The coach who was up front

Going over the stats with a portable lamp he carried
Asked us what was so funny to some guys who'd just
Lost by twenty-two points. It got quiet and our thoughts
Drifted toward the windows where time passed by,
Indifferent to the affirmations of eyes.

Dating a Law Student (1956)

She stood on Clarendon Street
Outside the apartment she shared
With two other women and listened
As he explained at good-humored length
Why he was ten minutes late:
His roommate, a misplaced favorite tie....

She looked into his beautiful
Gray-blue eyes, the color at once
Stern and soft, like mist at dusk on a lake.
She clutched hard at her pearl necklace.
She could see the boy inside the man,
The cautious pain and the wish to
Be dismissed, to go back to his childhood
Room and read a story or oil a mitt
Or patiently assemble a model plane—
The generous decency of privacy.

She thought she felt a chill in the warm
September night.
                    Two recent wars were over
But he'd had a father and been drilled.
"You needn't," she said as she moved
To kiss him, "be quite so accountable."
Her lips were slightly reddened, she
Could feel his eyes melt a bit.
The whole careful balance of her womanhood
Surged toward him—
An elaborate throbbing predicate.

He too leaned forward,
However deliberately.

They would dance at a country club
On hot summer evenings,
The air thick as jelly.
They would have several babies.
He had practiced carefully and so,
In her own mirrors, had she.

1914

August contracts imperceptibly the way a scab
   Wizens and frays. It will
   Finally fall into the still pool of September.

No huzzahing crowds gather nor do newspaper
   Banners shout dizzying threats.

Two lovers walk down a cart-worn lane.
They confide to one another little likes
   And dislikes they never before have said aloud.

Diaries record the depredations of rabbits,
   An older sister's trip to Paris,
   The price of butter, a gypsy encampment.

When people look in mirrors they see only
   Themselves in the unflappable fullness
   Of the beribboned or mustachioed moment.

No one winces at thoughts of what is
   To be accomplished next. Like a bolt
   In a slot the dry calendar clicks.

Dawn does not tremble; night does not shrill.

A steady hand writes a serifless script:
Twelve bushels of oats and a long conversation
With George about the vagaries of grapes.

No one listens extra carefully; no one bestows
In the middle of a meal a lingering look.

The lovers argue, the wheat rots, a little girl
    Begins to cry although her mama says
    With the calm wisdom of practiced years
    That it is only a fairy tale.

(for Andrey Gritsman)

The Blue Note

What seemed a great tide of years
Retreats, and the blue note
Insinuates itself, a small bird in
The early morning's dark throat

Making a small announcement.
I lie in bed and fear
Something, feel a blunt, arthritic throb.
You don't need a doctor to hear

A body's grief. It is unslurred.
The bird leaves off and the silence
Feels gracious and calm.
What post-Cartesian soul said, *Love indifference*

And you can love God? It begins
To brighten up outside,
A relentless infiltration from
Black to gray to the wide,

Rivery joy of daylight.
The pain recedes some. Weeds
Are pulled apart by sparrows
In their search for seeds.

MIA—Missing in America

The country western song begins
    Minor-key-beseechingly that
Little Jim's been gone for three years now
    And no one's heard a word,
That he's out there on the big road,
    Et cetera.

The music's too cozy the way most of
    The recent stuff is too cozy
For its own good. Hank Williams—to cite
    The retrievable past—could be plaintive steel
But the subject in any unmetaphorical
    Case is that

Prairie of starkness where though
    A man's getting out of bed in some room
Each morning the pride of purposefulness has fled.
    He didn't like his home
And whether they're dead or alive
    Is beyond him

And behind him, on another planet.
    Shee-it, as they say in some
Parts of the United Snakes, and what happens
    After a man loses his taste for bourbon
And one-night stands is aloneness like no
    Nashville mouth-full-

Of-good-teeth has a clue about.
    It's paying the month by the week and
Cashing checks in storefronts with a metal door
    Sporting three alarms and

It's looking into a few too many
    Eager faces

Ready to own how the truth is their relative
    And it's throwing a couple of duffel bags
Into the car and lighting a cigarette
    And leaving. Anywhere is somewhere
And the rancid fluorescence of one more
    All-night truck stop

Is the gospel of speed limitless darkness.
    A man's just doing his part as his
Mind travels back to high school and
    The "general" (means dumb) science class
He was in and the notion of molecules,
    These little particles

That made up big bodies but they
    Didn't know what they were doing,
They were unto themselves but somehow part
    Of things. Nothing could be without them.
What a family notion, he thinks, as he drives
    And turns the station.

Immolation (1964)

...and what I, as a raw, scoffing,
Know-it-all adolescent, saw in the photos
Was horror that had nothing to do
With movie screens but something for which
I mercifully had no words although
The feeling of that deliberateness,
Of going about the preparations to set oneself
On fire and the imagined actual moment of the match
Engulfed me for endless seconds in a dizzying
Dread so that when the toaster clunked
Or the coffeepot began to burble I looked up
And regarded them as if they were artifacts
Of the afterlife and I felt my sight no longer was
Human vision but the insight of unearthliness.
I then went on about my day and forgot
As we are prone to say when we remember
But what forgetting was there for anyone
Who looked however closely at that sight?
So that at times decades later I see
At random moments that photo-moment and begin
To think I can feel the courage that is not
The steeling, got-to-do-it sort (though that
Is no small thing) but a peace that comes
From feeling the violent hurt of humankind and not
Flinching or souring or even lamenting but
Stepping into the fire that is always there
And embracing it completely as
The odor of gasoline floods the nostrils
And the scratching match is calm thunder.
In that absolute moment of the lighting
Are all moments and I vow again
To shut my shifting mouth before the fire

And the life—so many moments—that disappears
Like wars or photos or the darkest,
Most acrid flames. The candor
Of suffering survives....

The Author

Baron Wormser is the author of four previous collections of poetry: *The White Words* (Houghton Mifflin, 1983), *Good Trembling* (Houghton Mifflin, 1985), *Atoms, Soul Music, and Other Poems* (Paris Review Editions, 1989), and *When* (Sarabande Books, 1997). His poems, essays, and reviews have appeared in a wide variety of journals including *The Paris Review*, *Sewanee Review*, *The New Republic*, *Harper's*, and *Poetry*. He has received fellowships from the National Endowment for the Arts and the John Guggenheim Memorial Foundation. He lives with his wife in Hallowell, Maine.

Dan Rodrigue